Published by Sourcebooks, Inc.
P.O. Box 4410, Naperville, Illinois 60567-4410
(630) 961-3900
Fax: (630) 961-2168
www.sourcebooks.com

Printed and bound in China.
LEO 10 9 8 7 6 5 4 3

Dear Readers,
Where and how do we dig for the
frequently-spoken-of "reservoir of inner strength"? A
map to lead us is so important, to provide a
starting place saying, "you are here." I hope this book
serves as a reminder that your personal "you
are here" can always be found in your heart.

Share your sparkle wherever you are.

—dodinsky

When you are looking at a mountain, marveling at its beauty and strength, realize it is looking right back and admiring you.

Embrace your own greatness.

Consider your heart a cocoon from which dreams emerge like butterflies to wander in the garden.

A mind preoccupied with thoughts of
resentment and bitterness cannot
change the past. Nor do those thoughts
wound anyone but the soul that beholds them.

Unbind your spirit.

Don't let the opinion of others restrain you.

I survived my insecurities and though
the road is daunting, I have learned being
true-to-oneself is good company.

If others want to define you, don't linger
in their pond. Swim away from their ignorance
and find your ocean.

Even if you find your voice,
sometimes it does not matter anymore,
when you speak to someone
who is deaf by choice.

I hope that when you count the stars, you begin with yourself.

May you embrace the moonlight with your dreams.

The horizon, to remind you of your
courage, sends its gentle waves
of confidence to kiss your feet.

Do not let your shadow walk you.
You are not a slave of the past.

When you go after your dreams,
sometimes the crowd yells its wishful thinking.
Ignore that explosion of opinion,
and follow the trail leading to your heart.
It will always whisper *your* truth.

The dreams of the broken are
mightier than the wishes of the dead.

Be there for others,
but never leave yourself behind.

When you own your imperfections and
you embrace your life, you become a better person.

Life is about turning obstacles into pedestals.

The strength of your will
cannot be imprisoned by
other people's ignorance.

Do not become a stranger to yourself by blending in with everyone else.

Your road to happiness should be memorable for the scenery as well as the destination.

When you stray away from your soul,
the distance you have traveled is
measured by the aching of your heart.

If you stumbled today,
remember where and how it felt.
Tomorrow, take a different path.

Life flourishes from its pain
and the lessons we gain.

When it seems that everything you do is wrong and everyone is against you—it is the best time to wear your "I-don't-give-a-damn" tutu.

Glide gleefully in the dance
floor of "this is me and my life."

If someone you trusted
betrayed you by choice,
don't cuddle up to the
rejection or blame yourself.
Why don't you pick yourself up
and love yourself better?
This, too, is by choice.

There is a place called happiness, it is just
an arm's length away from your fears and
a few steps beyond your misgivings.

To get there, sometimes
you need to take the path
of courage down to the
street of never-give-up,
until you reach the field of
dreams.

Dreams

Never give
up

courage

Misgivings

fears

Happiness

The question is not why they don't like you
when you are being you.
It is why you waste time
worrying what they think.

If you are not hurting anyone with your actions,
keep moving forward with your life.

Every morning I start with a drink
from my cup of sunshine, to remind myself
of who I am before I step into the world
of "this is who *we* think you are."

No matter how far the distance
you have traveled or the failures
that have gathered, hope would
still meet you anywhere.

It is time to go and leave the past behind. Exile the thoughts of painful memories.

You have learned what they have taught you.

I hope you see the luster in the simplest of things and heed the whispers of the heart.

After all, there is a part of you that knows that having less can mean living more.

The butterfly said to the sun,
"They can't stop talking about my
transformation. But I can only do it once
in my lifetime. If only they knew that
they can transform at any time
and in countless ways."

No one can dictate what attitude you will wear today. If you meet someone whose intent is to put you down, remember it is *you* who wears the crown.

Do not plant your dreams
in the field of indecision, where nothing
ever grows but the weeds of "what-if."

To be at peace, your opinion
of yourself must outweigh the
assumptions of others about who
you are. It is a conscious decision
that their words no longer have
the ability to keep you down.

Your value is the product of your thoughts.
Do not miscalculate your self-worth
by multiplying your insecurities.

They who do not fear darkness
have learned to light their own candle.

All the puzzle pieces are in your hands! Don't go looking for someone to complete it for you. That only reinforces the fear that you are incomplete. Life's strongest glue is being happy to be you!

Growing old with someone else
is beautiful, but growing old
while being true to yourself is divine.

A Doormat's Perspective

A muted existence
to anguish in silence,
it's nearly impossible
for the doormat
to find release.

I doubt if it knows
the key is hidden
right under it,
so very close,
always within reach.

The soul does not absorb negativity
by accident, only by choice.

Knowing who you are is
the best defense against
who they think you are.

There are friendships imprinted
in our hearts that will never
be diminished by time or distance.

Sometimes the one you dismiss so easily is the one who will stay to weather the storm with you.

To strengthen the muscles of your heart,
the best exercise is lifting someone else's
spirit whenever you can.

You cannot avoid bad days. Sometimes you
will shut a lot of doors, dimming your own light
and creating a mind-set of woefulness.

Although we are responsible for our own happiness, having a friend who opens more doors than you close is truly one of life's greatest blessings.

Do not worry about others leaving
you behind. They are not going
where you are headed.

It is not who finished first,
but who saw the most of life.

If you travel in a path that makes you
happy and you are misunderstood by many,
I hope you consider the opinion that
carries the most weight—YOURS.

You can't stop people from passing judgment. But they can't build your prison—you do.

A great many battles I have won are
those that I have walked away from.
They have strengthened my character,
helping me learn that, in life, it is not always
necessary to prove you are right.

Know that there are people you
can never please and questions
you simply don't need to answer.

I hope you know that who you truly are can never be replaced by who they imagined and wanted you to be.

Be grateful to those who left you,
for their absence gave you the strength
to grow in the space they abandoned.

When I reach the place
of my dreams, I will thank
my failures and tears.
They too, kept me going.

Acknowledgments

To my parents, Melba N. and Rustico N., who raised me with love and asked nothing but for me to be the best person I could be. To my friends, Arthur G., Carolyn B., Tracy H., and Sandra K., who served as fuel to my dreams and asked nothing but for me to keep on shining. To my agent, Wendy K. and editors Shana D. and Deirdre B., who believed in me and made this dream a reality. To my readers, who continue to engage with me and share my writings with family and friends: You validate what I do. Thank you all!

—dodinsky

A ton of gratitude to my parents Virginia and John (Dad, I know you're cheering for me up there!) for their love and encouragement. Many thanks to my dear siblings Nigel and Debbie for their support. And finally, thank you to my fans! Your kind compliments and general cheering-on have delighted and inspired me daily.

—Amanda

About the Author

At an early age, Dodinsky searched for life's meaning and came to see the world from a unique perspective. He recognizes the simplicity in the most complex situations, masterfully perceives the emotions involved, and from these, weaves words that inspire people's spirits.

About the Illustrator

Amanda Cass is a carefree spirit living in the glorious vineyards of Marlborough, New Zealand. Her mission is to help spread love, life, and freedom through her art.